APARIGRAHA

'CAUSE HOA ROT

JAYA CHAUDHARY

Copyright © Jaya Chaudhary
All Rights Reserved.

This book has been self-published with all reasonable efforts taken to make the material error-free by the author. No part of this book shall be used, reproduced in any manner whatsoever without written permission from the author, except in the case of brief quotations embodied in critical articles and reviews.

The Author of this book is solely responsible and liable for its content including but not limited to the views, representations, descriptions, statements, information, opinions and references ["Content"]. The Content of this book shall not constitute or be construed or deemed to reflect the opinion or expression of the Publisher or Editor. Neither the Publisher nor Editor endorse or approve the Content of this book or guarantee the reliability, accuracy or completeness of the Content published herein and do not make any representations or warranties of any kind, express or implied, including but not limited to the implied warranties of merchantability, fitness for a particular purpose. The Publisher and Editor shall not be liable whatsoever for any errors, omissions, whether such errors or omissions result from negligence, accident, or any other cause or claims for loss or damages of any kind, including without limitation, indirect or consequential loss or damage arising out of use, inability to use, or about the reliability, accuracy or sufficiency of the information contained in this book.

Made with ♥ on the Notion Press Platform
www.notionpress.com

Three cheers to society.

Contents

Foreword   *vii*

Preface   *ix*

Acknowledgements   *xi*

Prologue   *xiii*

In The Pantry Of Parenting

   1. Will Will Ever Be Willing A Life He Lives?   3

   2. Was I Painting The Petals Of Petroleum Coated Flowers?   7

   3. To Her Vintage Borders, That Ends At My Dockyard.   11

Women And The Ironical Cups

   4. Itra   17

   5. Marriages   21

   6. The Witchcrafting   24

   7. Yours Truly   26

   8. Buy Me A Coffin And Then Ahead To Read   27

   9. Badnaam Gali   28

   10. To The Hon'ble Sun From Some Scattered Candles   33

   11. Once Upon A Time, I Met A Future Rapist   34

   12. Ars Moriendi   38

   13. To Dust-holic Almirah And Chirpy Window Panes   41

The Adulting Franchise

   14. Zing-girl Bells   47

   15. Doors.   50

   16. Undress Hopes   53

   17. Hi College Days   56

   18. Loneliness   59

   19. Have You Ever Been Drenched In Tension Of Desperate   63

Contents

Rains?

20. If It Were My Last Poems — 66

21. Nothing Hurts Me Anymore — 68

How May I Put This?

22. Immortal Death — 73

23. Bloated Letters — 75

24. How May I Put This? — 76

Ageing Climbers

25. Woods By Lake — 81

26. Epiphany Is Waiting — 82

27. Can You Sing Me Some New Metaphors Please? — 83

28. Balls And Chains — 84

29. Sublimed Graves — 86

30. In Standstill Backwaters Of Past — 89

31. Farehenheit — 91

32. Death — 93

Aparigraha — 99

Foreword

Jaya is a brilliantly perceptive writer whose words can be felt deeply within. Her writings reflect the shaping of selfhood. Her vibrant metaphors are sometimes razor-sharp and other times a soothing touch of dew. She knows the worth of language and articulates her truth in such a fantastic fashion that it renders one speechless.

-Esha Yadav (Close Friend, India)

Jaya likes to pen down experiences in prose form. Her imagery is solid and she paints a picture with her words. Some of her work is extremely strong and forces one to take a moment away to breathe, which proves the fact of her work is beautiful but tough.

- Deepanshu Jaiswal (Close Friend, India)

Jaya is one of a kind writer.
She's something whose content speaks for itself. Her work is bold and powerful while keeping the literary elements intact, she inculcates expressions so beautifully in her writings that it reaches the right place. One will be in awe, with the way she jots down her writings!

-Devguni Singh (Close Friend, Avid Reader, India)

Jaya goes by the pen name Jaggery. She is the writer/poetess, I find soothing to read at times. She fascinates me with intricacies she adds in the small incidents. The zeal for writing critically speaks of the unjust social norms which also is one of my favorite thing to read of her.

- Vivek Sharma(Close Friend, Reader, India)

Jaya, symbolises Victory, and her writing exemplifies the same. With her words she conquered her past, constraints, emotions and experiences. And this work is her great conquest!

- Kshama Mishra(Close friend, Reader, India)

Preface

Imagine this scenario, where on a particular day, You wake up and walk into this long beautiful, coffee shop with a fat cabin and voluminous aroma of positivity. You sit in there all happy and chattering about how nice the entire ordeal of the place is and how it fits into the description of your perfect place. You treat the staff there in a very nice way. You are thrilled by the menu card, all your favorite delicacies at the right affordable price with no compromise in taste. Fascinated to listen to anecdotes of people growing together from *since forever* to *till forever*. You love the place, you take your friends and family there. You gradually form relationships there. Strangers become friends who drop you home and pick you up and celebrate your important dates and then you have your bad days when you shout at one of your friends. You start coming alone as if to hide from the mess you created both in the past and present. You find comfort in its warm and loving environment and then you start to hate it. You recall all the times you fought with a loved one and confided in the corner seat of the cafe and felt weak, crippled by your endearing personality. You avoid looking back at the place you once loved. You gradually grow out of it and find another place where you can never smell coffee again or see the brown cabin with cute posters or bread rolls at the same price. You would find things tastier, costlier, and more affordable or worse but never the same, but still, you would avoid the cafe at its best.

The cafe has seen it all. The lovers, who promised *forevers,* now burn down the memories by calling the cabinet, they visited for two years, fat and ugly. The cheaters, who sway in and out of the hinge doors more often than anybody else wearing wigs and different hands with sugar-scented promises rasped in artificial roses. The moods, with aristocracy on the nose and blue hands of humanity to soak in the sobs of those who are now once upon a time. The friends, playing smile and sniff from under many skins. The perfect families, always disappointed and grumbling over the minute of dissemblance. The imperfect families, with kids without a front tooth and pale skin to celebrate the elder child's annual report with all that they got, grateful and polite. The daughters in love, smiling the pearly white teeth at strangers she would marry. The daughters out of love, bargaining just the right of *dahej* would do. The happy wives, with husbands away on borders, and sad wives with husbands collapsing on wrong ends. Last but not the least, the hypocrites, addressed as writers, promising to never return and now share anecdotes in the cafe's name.

What do you relate to more? Being the person who once had a cafe or the cafe itself, who is accustomed to meeting people when they need them. I am that hypocrite writer, writing in the name of Cafe.

Acknowledgements

This book is like the trampoline of all I have observed closely. I would like to extend my grateful thanks to my parents, I am not an easy child but this love I get is just so profound. At the end of the day, I love you both as my providers, you both showered me with nothing less than the best. I am blessed to belong to you both. My teachers, and the entire LPS family from 2005-2018. My group Esha, Deepanshu, Prabhat, Saumya, Sakshi, and Shashank, I love you guys for an eternity now. A special thanks to my adorable readers Devu didi, Vivek, Sarthak, and my little brother Gaurav who have been around me like a constant push to complete this work. I am also grateful for the presence of all the helping hands in my life who make my life so much easier. Not to forget my baby sister, Juhi, who is like my backbone and trust me one of the best readers, one day when I was reading "Crime and Punishment" she comes up and asked me the name of the writer of the book and I told her about Fyodor Dostoevsky, and that the book was a classic. Once she acknowledged the fact that the writer is long dead, she was so disappointed, she said, "Its so bad that a writer dies, I mean you can read all the books they have written but you also know that they are not going to write a new book ever again." I felt it like she has such a vivid picture of things.

No matter how much we have normalised bad mental health, cherishing small things is another major missing. Only after shifting to this so gorgeous, apparently free life I realised, the presence of all my friends and family in my life is a blessing. Thank you so much to each and every one who have contributed to this beautiful life and tried their best to keep me happy. I mean every single of you who have made efforts in one or the other way. I am grateful, very grateful and my words can never comply with the feelings and amount of respect I hold for all of you. Thank you very much for simply

ACKNOWLEDGEMENTS

existing.

Prologue

The book is a fictional work of art dealing with the residuals of bad days and emotions that follow in the aftermath. Besides, the phase of letting go and looking up to new beginnings, the book also encapsulates major mental health issues, including chaotic households, harassment, child abuse, and other triggering subjects. The book redirects the idea of opening the fist of emotions and unfolding it one by one.

I have tried my best to evoke the emotion of accepting one's own mistake and taking accountiblity for them is a major part of healing. With my little understanding of the world, I have tried to put myself in various scenarios and put before you all, my very best work.

In the pantry of Parenting

Growing up is a prayer song, repeated every day like sunrise.

1. Will Will ever be willing a life he lives?

the clock hung in the middle of whole numbers
and *Will* rolled the curtains while on his way
to reach out for an undecided subject in the backpack of
Tuesdays.

The afternoon sun burnt his rosy cheeks and windows had no sign of women, who would accompany mother on evening walks.
an hour would pass looking at the frozen pages while he strolled along the kitchen with dancing smiles,
all in his mind.

> *"Will would wonder what neurons make him laugh when wars are over and the villain dies, should he laugh at all?"*

the forgotten pages of the neuro system would shift adjusting themselves with the flow of preoccupied air,
and the hall chirped with the ***do's and don'ts*** for Will to register.

> *"it's about time and I will bring Utopia to life*
> *singing charades and gulping the leftover*
> *dessert down my throat to go back forever*
> *to unlabelled land of muses"*

When mother used to leave closing the door behind her,

APARIGRAHA

I wondered if she thought of what I do at home
if I sat at the window edges just so I find it better to study
or if mother knew I guarded the doors of <u>her presence,</u>
whilst talking to a friend I had never seen, he laughed along peacefully,
I presumed he didn't live in the same home as me.

"*How could he ever?*"

He didn't tell me to focus on **empty plates** while eating
or to (un)hear the **conversation of wills** where the Will wasn't me.
He <u>played along and clapped</u> in the air when I won two battles in a row.
He <u>danced to my music,</u> though I was conscious of how he really thought of them
since **he didn't speak**,
I always hoped it was good to listen to
unless one day mother told
me my voice screeched.
though he sat in the audience attentively and always, I didn't sing any further
and he didn't persist.
He didn't grumble about how untidy my room was as I clean along;
he reminded me of a child I once was.
Looking at the corners of the room while mother cleaned it,
wiping the <u>crestfallen stories</u> off the window panes,
both inside out and still when mother used to talk of wills,
it wasn't me.
it was never me.
He never ate either, I swallowed jars of jellies

scraping every bit off the moist leads that covered it.
He would look at me holding one spoon after other
till I dropped one and we would wind up the noodle plate altogether.
The empty moist wash basin was a sign of **doomsday** for kids like **me**
left behind to study in one's room so ***he would fan the wet sinkholes***
dry and leave behind <u>no stains of quarrel in cabins</u> preoccupied.
He was a good teacher and often told me I was his favorite, quite a few times.
I cried a few times before him, though he couldn't hug me even if he tries to
which reminds me of a long list of lovers, friends and family who wished to hug me.

> "*-if only wishes were dropped on trampolines and I were the whole sky-*"

How beautiful were the days when no one was home,
we played <u>understanding</u> on dinner tables and television halls,
where what I have to watch, eat, listen to and wear mattered equally.
Nevertheless at a point of time when
Loneliness took off its slippers at door,
I waited for the doorbell to ring so as to
make him, *my friend* stay a little longer
saw it fading through the doors,

> "*-and bite me, 'cause it hurt and I can't buy any ointment to mend both our pains, besides waiting for night to wake up when he returned wearing night lamps looking at me while I slept and he didn't.*"

and while growing up he'd ask me what I would ever be,
I told him I will be him,
because he was so profound
like still water allowing the boat to disturb its calmness,
still never losing its character.
like fathers attending **PTMs** of there average son,
accepting and cheerful.
like attentive mothers holding hands of there fat daughters and toothless son
caring and possesive.

> "*-when he turned eighteen with me, he didn't return after one fine day.*"

and on the attic I had my present,
Silence
silence, was his name.
and I am grown up.
*and I am **him** now, like I said.*
like I wished.
I am him now, <u>silent</u>.

2. Was I painting the petals of petroleum coated flowers?

petroleum- viscous, glossy, waterproof.
Springs are too spoiling to keep a poppy from blooming,
it eventually does.
with the serendipity of his glossy gaze, melting away the winter locks.
It blooms.

> *"So it did to me."*

My niche isn't art, it isn't the pollen either,
it isn't in the volume of how much brown and how much wet
and in February, when I left the slambook unpainted,
the forlorn garden and the stone hedged post box bit me
three bites of nostalgia with a carnivorous spine
of <u>death, a delay, and a delusion.</u>
In the evening, when I shouldn't have,
I walked barefoot on the mud-lined pavements
leading to a hierarchical Supermarket.
I followed the steps, some in snickers,
some in dots of very standard heels,
some others disappearing in sanitary stores.

> *"Babumoshai, this heart doesn't chew naphthalene when out in search of aroma."*

The long benches had some cruel labels

APARIGRAHA

like reviews that watchman forgot to take down
and my fingers crawled into the wrong vessel out of habit.
acrylics of do-not(s) dripping drop by drop and adsorbing
every bit of my green breeches
it battled its way upwards
carefully lynching the cotton from within
too aware of the denim's blue.
The pastels, the brushes and sketch rolls,
bottled in a pile, too costly
but it's fine, no?
When the price is some bitcoins earthed out of
narrating fairy tales.
The bags hence packed, stuffed, and dripping the drops
of forbidden fun
for the upcoming protagonist to follow.
Off to the nursery, though my cell phone rings twice,

> "*I am sorry maa, you won't understand
> how many choices I am yet to rejoice!*"

She told me twice not to visit the florist,
but it is like buying the first cover of some cliche show,
that one has read over a hundred times and yet again.
so why not?
when *fire sprawls you blame the fingers, the cigar, and its owner*
never the wind, the kerosene, or the matchstick, why?
I battle the pedals till they giveaway before the nursery
upon some red carpets that don't hurt.
I still couldn't bandage the eyes

that meander gaze after gaze into my teen legs.
I stand up and make my way to the flocks of daisies and chrysanthemums'
and pluck the roots away till the freshness of wet mint stitch my hands
into syllables of green rains, devour the warmth of all pain ever born.
I collect a little lot of seeds and feed them to the paddles
to recover soon and *help me reach a place called home, in time.*
The heavy long paint log,
Floods your backyard and sneak in silently,
planting the lips of every root, digging deeper, and scratching the
silent fast asleep mud.
Wrapping the roots and seeds together and caressing the flowers.
I sit cross-legged pensive about what to paint now
waiting for freckles to turn into messy buns
of wedlocks in my mind to key the divorce.
I disarm my eyes of glitters, saline, and scarlet
beside the moonlit ivory petals of some tongue-twisting flower.
the mosquitoes still anticipate the lower back and upfront and everywhere,
but sleep makes me dead,
and I sleep soaking wet in the rain.
<u>The morning sobers your wetness and the sun smiles at me,</u>
<u>the colors are gone,</u>
<u>The dress is green and white again,</u>
<u>the denim not to forget chewed by the moisture of the night.</u>
Everything is gone,
the seeds, the cycle, the florist
and the wound that mint healed,
girls are out of the supermarket

and I too, walk out with them plainly.
holding paper wrapped poly bags, and
I still see the other lane and I still plan on mischieves
I **could** never do.

> "*acceptance is the red sauce of drama and denial is the red wine, the age is the factor and my story ends there.*"

3. To her vintage borders, that ends at my dockyard.

Tall, whimsical hair in french curls.
sit in apricity blocked by five trees
in a row and each of them now
has a story to hide.
First,
hides leaf of autumn where
Grandma rolls the thread into a spinning wheel of happiness
and the cat person spies the woolen yarn
for suspended winters.
The school forms rest on coffee tables
with paperweights stopping the winds
to take them to a home unknown.
The moral is not to leave the paperweights
unguarded or tell the yarns of upcoming cats.
Second,
hides the mud in shoes while stirring the icy lumps
mother told not to swallow in any go,
the story witnesses a bleaching tail of how fear grows from
sticks of nonchalance to the punctuality of buying a notebook every day
and pen down how greasy hands untied the laces of auburn lights
in oil pastels between warm hands.
Certain times moral is just to see and paint the same sky
in colors of hidden leaves.

Third

is cruel to weep occasionally to people about how broken the kneecaps get

and all you witness is the monologue of winds swaying the mad branches

clapping the forgotten swings in the air.

I wonder if he missed her sitting upon the roots with a carpenter's bag or how she walked away with her bag packed empty enough to fill seeds for the next borders.

Fourth,

flattering mirrors of strength

glued with rejections of fragrant lovers walking in and out like

post it on empty refrigerator doors of a forgotten room where

you look out for cerelac at nights when an empty stomach

reminds you how lovely summers could be

if a fresh breeze had a haircut of its own

flowing tastefully through the twirls of now stagnant feet.

Feet frozen in the mornings of a bushy ground looking back at the garland of borders it made

off to buy seeds for borders from a shop of yellow aesthetics.

Fifth,

Grasping rains and thunderstorms, calmest of all and a masterpiece in making, shortest as of yet and yet the tallest of all.

tallest in terms of hows over whys

a hoodie should circle the arms and warm the periphery of fantasy under soft skin,

of when to plant another border insightfully and how not to tell the world

those plastics do not shiver when tensile is compared they rather skip the test.

And on Christmas, it's good to hang the bottles of liquor upside down just so the roots' capacity to absorb toxins saturates and burst open in orbs of

skywalking cupcakes.

And then when we meet over a blank space, you'll press enter to tell me how beautiful your eyes look because I made you cry.

and now I tell, you how sad you were and toxins turned into orbs just in time.

Women and the ironical Cups

<u>how many slurps would help you realise, the mug is empty, or it was never filled in the first place?</u>

4. Itra

there is a kanestar of paraffins and scented wood,
which leaks a lot of farmyard letters
about the tiffin boxes she delivered to the wrong address.

"This is like a fairytale, once upon a time."

in the age while I still dial wrong numbers on purpose
she placed the unsigned letters addressed to her approxi-mate,
and folded them in neat plates.
She would cover them with foliage at the edges and sprinkle
Itra
to reassure her armpits that they don't stink
because **sweat swallows the epiphany of love.**
She applies mustard oil to the
folds of sensible chuckling french tales that are heavy enough to sink
in the pond
and yet not die.
<u>She stuffs sugar smothered saunf simply</u>
to avoid the aftermath of thick emulsions.
and wait for the scoundrel with whiskers and not moustaches, already
white
and the baby boy, twice her age to sit with the taller leg resting on the
heavier one
and moustache whitewashed in sawdust.
and leftover mehndi graze upon

his bald head.
it was just the next day,
she did not wait for the bus stand,
stapled the sides of her flowing dupatta
or mentioned the direction of the key to anyone.
She picked up her kanester
folded its hands into a monopoly of scrunchies
holding her bun and varmala together
at some distance with the nuptial.
She packed the white sport shoes too,
but the drill between bedrooms and kitchen
is on <u>*platform heels*</u>
till cribs come and then its all barefoot
and the caravan leaves behind the burdens.
She redunants a few laughter after aeons of
sleeping and walking and cooking thirst
she finally wakes up one new moon day,
<u>*and smiles briskly a quarter and a half smiles.*</u>
<u>*looking at her features, growing younger again.*</u>

༻❦༺❦༻❦༺

On occasional nights when a white swarm knits sweaters of her feathers
in the dark corner of the
a spongy seat, she sits smiling and clapping in the air
reliving, the puppet show,
with **live dolls and rehearsed conversation.**
She would walk back with naked hands and a jiggling side bag,
placing conversation of happiness on your cutlery

just when a door knob will open wide and shut again
in **oblivion.**
With stitched pockets and buttons right in place,
he has no questions about how many ink pots you will need more
to complete your latest poem,
and *he did not even know you wrote one.*
it's her talking about the random doorbells and how many time
it is not the delivery boy.
she smelled the raw string of her broken instruments and it still sings her
song of wet matka days.
Upon green tablelands with a lot of breezes to pack
lilacs to home.
which she now plants in your tiny fingertips alternatively
and she hates that
they smell like tobacco.
and when you **drip fingers with porcelain blood,**
she knows which wrong number called again
and which cup hit the edge of iron beds.
she lets you *handle the candles*
also looks at you melting the wax on your scarred hands
and knows who is the reason for your vapourized diyas.
look close she did not wear the saree with the same folds
or planted teenagers again, did she?

> "*When you look at cyclone after cyclone, in your
> little life, what she does might be the epilogue
> of some unsung tragedy,
> she smiled and covered itra under*

the plastic papers over the shelves you always found neat. "

She talks, and tries to be happy on days like when you meet her,
and when you
rest your buttered body on her left arm,
and the cell phone beeps,
taking *you out of reach from her periphery,*
she looks at the kanester,
and **saudade smiles at her from some distance.**
The door knob opens and draws the curtain
she weaves the climax of her tales.
where she chose a choice that doesn't matter to you,
but binds you into a suit of happiness.
that's how she was taught and that is how she will teach you,
to roll a small sphere of dough on the pastor board
and forget that you have to laugh
with a positive voice in your windpipes.

"So, an Ardhangini sits every Saavan under the tall tamarind trees,
till one day a crow approves of the
visitors.
and this tale is bygone, but I still find the empty bottles of itra in the
outskirts of my village, under tamarind trees.
"

5. Marriages

At cockcrow, she veiled the burning sensation
behind the eyelids
and her daemon would lose the grip of
her sighs.
<u>Smiling half-naked teeth,</u>
<u>rest are too red to distinguish from</u>
<u>the equal red lips and tongue</u>

> *"a cup of tea slams the door into her eyes"*

breaking a cartilage or two.
The carpets shifts in uneasiness
and the elbow that held her clad skin slips
flat on the soft cotton bed.
curtains and windows will swing enough,
jumbling the gaping air
for her gossamer lips to sink in a smile
and would go silent
blaming themselves for the vacuum they added.

> *"They heard it all, all that he didn't."*

The few hairs, enough to be braided into three strands of lies,
collapse a flex of question on her blank face.
a loose scrunch of deep red will look back at her
like a petition she defiled.

She looked at it and it looked back,
for an hour they met for the last time
<u>and she drops her hope off the floor,</u>
<u>both drowned in June fever.</u>
The hot floor and aching hope crawled side by side and fiberglass hugged its moans with a screeching cry.
the toothbrush would laugh at its loneliness and reflection would kiss her wheatish cheeks from behind,
tossing the toothbrush into the voluble face of the giant open-mouth jar,
she would rinse the bun with an air of silicates packed in the pockets of her hand and punch her eyes balls with swathes of scented aloe vera.
She heard the fragments of her defeated bone, each speaking a different identical anecdote, with clichés one every count of three attempts. They won't shut till the frozen lakes don't freeze them.
Waiting for a waterfall to wash the <u>blue depressions</u> and<u> black holes </u>of her collar bones,
but pessimistic skin cells are impermeable.
She must have thanked the body wash to wipe off the amylase stuck in the
ruptured blushes of her clavicles and fancy femur.
She cemented the cemetery of temples, with red lipsticks, labeled vermilion
and fed the dead authorities of a porcelain red breast
with a sequin silver blouse, when the decaffeinated whispers returned,
Speaking of the endless battle of darkness and attempts to vacuum, please.

> "The solitary brocade of her red saree sheepishly hid and still hid the fingerprints of death on her body.
> and she is herself smiling in syllables of her
> Parmeshwar's name."

<u>But this poem is not about her, it's about me,</u>
it's about the cornered eyes that rest upon my dusky skin settling the bargains over
my coffee color cheeks,
though dark will still be smitten and how proudly they say,

> "My son never looked up a woman,
> where 'he sure will molest one whilst sustaining the sunshine on the pallet of glittered hope and crush her prayers of white horse' remains
> silent."

But my dad and his dad and their wives and their elder daughter are all painting the walls
with an origami of planes made out of the sample papers,
I charcoaled and inked to satisfy the application of qualifications of an educated,
plus two unemployed candidates at a matrimonial website.
<u>How when your first daughter dies of electricity, you think twice to buy the second, a Physics book, but think nothing even when a million pyre woods are in ashes.</u>

> "Those who often bad mouth others,
> often ask for permission and sign them with green fingers in denial."

6. The witchcrafting

Fixing shoelaces in arrogant holes, she stood before the pink sky and smirked at the victory on her brown lips of dark red lipstick. She runs every day. Every day to snatch prey, who is singing charades before a woman draped in silk saree and cotton earrings. She swallows the sweat on her upper lip to play **Ghar-Ghar** from the bricks of a broken castle. When She returns with her feet swinging in burrowed arms and her black hemoglobin with ultra-smooth white skin, churning air in between the panting thighs of an equally ugly old man. The man with an utterly misled childhood and seminars of pearly outrageous blood-suckling witches.

The witch sits with preoccupied thoughts in her body. The witchcraft lab, with loathsome zombies drooling over the swaying, pointed noses and chins. The long fingers pointing fisted hands and the award ceremony walking right in place. The blue and black and red and maroon jealousy rolling down her flexes with every cascading ripple of her gothic hair which hides the grey skull of collapsing wits.

Potions after potions of, Green for wits, Yellow for charisma, and Pink for beautiful walks along the esophagus, already a breeding ground of molds and puked food. The potions toil hard day and night, borrowing life for themselves but somehow they can't outnumber the deaths weaved inside the latex of a stinking trachea.

The chewing gums burning into yeast and the samples of all different DNA swallowed in pamphlets of "we won't see each other again." create gasometric centers in the middle of a corpsified wishbone, equally like a beauty sleep without breathing. The moles around the lips stand tall like stamp-post telling the details of how far you stand from bad breaths of an ugly aftertaste, but they look beautiful as crafted by the spell.

Eventually, the potion has to die someday, it is better if it dies after the hair fall reveals the ugly weeping brain cells crawling like sloths in want of existence. Alas, born with a meager life-supporting system, and a strong destroying one. Never mind the potions die after a point of time when the slogs are bewildered and swallow the tears of a manipulative cause. Tears after hallucinating, a "Grand get together" at the ballroom when the witch only tasted the second-hand wines from several lips and sometimes tongues in a row.

The older the casting spells get, the feeble becomes its flame and the outcast becomes the recipient. And tantrums that gamble at fingers and clinking wine glasses erode down the shaft chewed lips discarded like the latex of gum tree under sophomore tables hiding the drooling dishes of the already dead ugly witch.

The witch, incomplete, devastated, and sloppy with the broken twigs of her magical brooms, now sits with adhesives carving fictitious canines and weeping over telepathy lines. Painting toes in black and black moles to peach, watching magic spells at "mirror mirror on the wall." and lynching on the words of a sunflower with the flesh of a human being.

7. Yours truly

Chapels were ready to unwind
a sober life soaked in morphine
of delicate love just a sip of your lips
to survive on them ever after.
The baskets, and the sepals in them,
were mocking the petals
to be fetish and frail before
my sanguine blush behind white veils.
Table salts to taste and fairylands to happiness
looking at the entrance
for another tale to begin
ascending steps of milestones in togetherness.
Many tuxes went in and went out
wearing hands of white garlands
to sob in touches of melancholy
and dance on violin nights.
with swears of never-ending love,
I still look at the entry
and polish my cheeks with borrowed blush,
brush after brush every hour
and another choking my eyes
with **little dark mascaras** and **fear-lynching lipsticks**
that breach my mind and promise my heart
that you will take me to the exit too,
and stitch the broken promise back to life.

8. Buy me a coffin and then ahead to read

Buy me a coffin and then ahead to read

The morning woke us in chapels exchanging rings and savouring lips with bread crumps dipped in wine.

Afternoon fetched us basking in each other's wild fantasies Groaning pains, pleasures, sharing exquisite elixir.

The sunset brought monotonous changes, fragile weakness on holds, frequent switching of pitches and silent dead gazes.

For my sake, I planned my dinner, including barbiturates in ingredients. With there topping and stuffings I lick the odour in food.

Now before the rays kiss my inflated self, pack me up and tune me to the longest sleep to infinity.

Sleep the shortest you can, for you ought to repeat the afore said nasty chores again

9. Badnaam Gali

"to love perhaps is sleepwalking in the linen of lies."

Sitara always said,
when she listened to my every story
until **_she became one._**
Before I could ever decide,
if it was the fault of fatal black, fidgeting blue, or tarnished red,
to love the mahogany skin of my Sitara,
she would wear *palm oil*
so that scars stare me evergreen
and she could name each one of them a "birth-mark".

"Are birthmarks still birthmarks if arriving after fifteen years of birth?"

Every time Grant road station would arrive,
she would bring her head into alignment with her spine,
an empty visage stuffed with salty goodbye
steals her from me
<u>before darkness hugs her with a consolation prize.</u>
Not enough is left to wonder about,
but every time she rests her unkempt hair
on my mild wet humid shoulders,
I fear a drop of tear would
soak my collared chiffon suit,

unraveling the crops of foreseen rumors.
It always felt heavier when she lifted
her sedimented head
without decanting anything at all.
She always stuttered into next-times,
if I told her to walk me home
until every time since forever.
Of the Cinderella I talk, was always late for first class
and left festival nights even before the
flyers melted into the damp grounds.
She colored her lower lip which appeared fuller
like waning moon
A mystery, she was layered in folds of
the foundation I never felt.
Raghav mocked her once in the corridor
and I thought it was perhaps
out of habit, unless.

> "*That charcoal night, like*
> *the one when you can*
> *feel tenebrous smoking on your skin.*"

I mounted my *chaalni*, a little over my head
and gaze a little deep into the ground.
I called her at the Grant road station
Once,
Twice
Thrice
and no more.

She was there, Sitara was there.
or maybe she wasn't.
It was just some as people called her Chandani
on a moonless night
Illuminating through a radiant scar of beauty
that resembled my Sitara.

"She was Chandani, until she wasn't."

Of words, I don't know,
were erupting on my lips but
a painful vacuum
gripped my neck
the very way she was strangling the pillar
Standing with her weight against it
as if to kill every last streetlight
that led to her no-name lane.

*"Jalpariyaan toh kitabo me khub bikti hai saheb,
Kabhi malad me mile toh daam puch ke aayiega."*

Her beautiful eyes were
perfected a lot like
black smoky chandelier
socketed with
a melting red candle.
*Her cheeks were breathing
errands of
Smiling,*

Swelling
Sobbing
in turns with slaps of her beholder.
I know not when
the traffic stopped
or if I said Sitara out too loud.
But it made sense what Sitara used to tell
the Chauffeur on those Friday evenings

> "*We often build homes in bodies we don't own and then name them mine.*"

Words were forming and deforming
on my tongue with
every bit of air I tried to suck in.
and her hands were revolting her palms
into fingers of lethal men
neverending in line.
and flashbacks of her telling me the
morbid tales of
Princess who died of tight laces
and parallax errors of futile fame.
She doesn't stop even
when her bleeding pink wrist rusted red
like an old wine.

> "*Coincidentally the night ended for me,*
> *though it didn't for her*
> *and I feel*"

her gaze resting upon my shoulders
Or searching for me in the college annual books, maybe trying the cellphone,
that was broken in the hustle of epiphany that night,
or maybe she never knew me at all.
I was just a sob story of lovers for her till
Western line, platform 4, Grant Road Station.
Maybe all of them who have kissed her hands
and blistered her bruises, I am one of them.
They all disappear after causing bruises
I disappeared to cause one.
But I don't know how to tell her
I love her still
not telling her hurts me,
Telling her would hurt her.
She trusted me with the truth, she never
wanted me to discover.

> "*Is it perhaps easy to love a lover who live lives for both you and themselves individually?*"

10. To The hon'ble Sun from Some Scattered candles

With the dieing sunshine,
I arise
It melts me gradually
to see it die,

By the moonlight
I flicker
and the shades of me turn bright

and with you to come again
I freeze
hiding my corpse
by the funeral

and then that eve
A new me
plays again
The fairyland fire game.

11. Once upon a time, I met a future Rapist

with waking whispers of misogyny,
I saw the grey sky lit by the dim-witted
celestial candle.
My eyes were cluttered with cobwebs and sand,
also, my yawning cave wouldn't shut up.
the scathed grinders would blabber their grudge,
and against hillock onions with sour green tomatoes
smashing icy chilies down its throat.

> "*The right hand of a sincere housewife
> would teach it manners so that it may not puke
> the ugly taste of gingers on rich white walls.*"

and swallow the paste which makes it exist
and beautiful.
The rocking chairs
with unbalanced sugar and constipated flushes
create another turbulence
in rock bed of caffeine that hits
the perspiring shores of my mother's temple.
for another hour while I scrub my teeth and brush my hair.
the chair arms would deliberately swing over the cleavage of dead victims
and the tongues of tall women.

The screeching noise of brakes would stop right in face of the greedy lustrous building
and **a little brat would suffocate an empty upside glass immersed in bell jar water.**
that's battling for breath and **he would punch in its face till it flips and drowns.**
you never know when men grow into abusers,
and glasses into beautiful women.

"*It's him.*"

I settled with swathes of an uneducated sheet of paper and a spoilt pen.
The literate archaic hardcover was about to teach when the principal of some famous school
popped the plate full of hot meals over a dress full of dried eyes.

"*The stigma of masculine hands is hereditary.*"

the clattering shoes reverberated with the sighs of four walls.
I know not of ears, but doors have an eye.
We all grow in age and numbers, girls become teenagers, and brats become boys.
house becomes palace
and one beside my library
was rich
so front yard grew into a water pool, gradually.
with large ribs and broad shoulders, he stood
clad, wearing unconscious eyes scanning the lean legs
the no hair embarrassment stitches knives and blades
to his to do list.

the wheatish skin that pronounced freedom
making circles in the overdressed pool,
sweating the noises of flapping water, and looking forward to running away into the ocean.
Alas! **The palace ponds have to end at a point.**
and the water hits harder there, harder than any boulder can.
braids are meant to be softer so when you slide your fingers into them,
it should hurt.
He had a set of parents, unlike others.
One was a **dad-dad** and the other was a **mom-dad**,
yang-yang and no summer breeze.
The softness of an oily face or the calmness of
seashore that overwhelms the coast and talk of empathy.
hiding a small chess set under the large
cabinets
and wrapping chess board's ears,
So that they may not whisper his name to his dad,
in the game of hide and seek.

> "*This is an anecdote*
> *that your grandmother won't tell because she is the victim*
> *in there and we all look through*
> *filters like despising the*
> *watermelon seeds we all swallow*
> *because they contain no cyanide.*"

At the edges, I still saw him
at a theatre, admiring others clap when the

girl said no for long
and married **the soft bed which was hard on her a few nights ago.**
He had company with him for his age. It was genuine but the smile wasn't.
I guess it's alright
but, looking at her, who walks an elegant catwalk with a pastel smile,
tall legs, and a little loose crop top
hides both the argument of a nine-inch belly and the cold hands of the same handsome man that walks her out.
Defeated by the battles,
I planned a revival wind tour.
and to my disaster, I heard two people talking,
in the corner plucking grass and I stopped by
placing my magic broom against the coconut tree and like always, his friend replied, *"sometimes a no means yes, and sometimes a maybe"*
It was him.
and I think of my dad, who still rocks upon his rock-hard chair,
jam-packed with newspapers that
tell other news written with **the best performance of chauvinists.**

12. Ars Moriendi

"where it ends, let's begin from there."

Like palaces. Like vaults.
like riches, like secrets for riches to prevail.
What hides behind the porcelain doors,
wait summers to campaign in furnace of secrets,
which is when we speak of
<u>Death, the tragic ones.</u>
Evenings begin at sunset, it's sleep that makes it night.
and that is when we hope to kiss sunshine, again.

"*what do you do when you're short of threads,*
And the cloak runs wide along the palace lines?"

"*we curve the needles and makes two knots in place of five,*
At a distance where threads agree,
we stitch a butterscotch smile."
"

So she does, Chavi.
and the threads that were supposed to *die of suffocation, die early at some distances.*
with the medals of surreal stitches in their name.
~
What do the maidens, and the queen, and the chapels and the prince?

What do the garlands, what do to the ceilings, what do I and what do you do?

Why do the banesters hide vaults after vaults? What smiles the Queen, when she wears a heavy eyelid above the wet eyelids? What stands for the castle? What stands against? What lures the grasses and what consumes the drops of rains upon our earth ? What O' Grandma, you breathe in the sand, and the sugars you taste smells like salt? What O' Grandma is this eve all about, when claps are thunderous and whispers of reality doom in them? What cheers the blossoms to never and every time bloom again? Is it a parody of disaster from one of the fictions the court writer wrote, or was it a forecast?

"*-d-e-b-r-i-s-*"

and all lay silent like *horizontal bottles*
with a wine glass nearby, sober enough to dress in dirt and hold the umbrellas high against
The never upcoming sun?
The brownness is so thick that borders don't stand a chance to dress red,
Brown gown
Brown turbans
Brown brocades
Brown dust
and red ground with night calling upon.
Stars appear to twinkle faster and faster and teeth grind a handful of crunchy sand and in the little distance flickers the uncovered orange in the middle of air, with silhouettes walking dead.

> "*Charm me O young princess, how you drape stargazing lilies into chrysanthemums and hope to get a bouquet of smiling daisies?*
> *Not all princesses become Queen, O' darling! Some marry vampires with castles that need no bottle opener, neither a watchman to guard the hallucinated gates.*"

So says honey, and kiss my nerves with
thirty knives and vows of vermillion death.
and tear me open,
unwinding the cap, and I freeze to sleep,
While he dwell the red wine and the siren discards the empty bottles back to dustbin cans,
called "p~o~s~t~m~o~r~t~e~m"

13. To dust-holic almirah and chirpy window panes

New birds growing at ghats where washermen's women
arrange trinkets whilst the water waves
walk past the bangles adding flavors to
4 AM breaths.
breaths smoking air
in the midnight fields of elephant grass
and earthworm grounds,
marshy enough to swallow white soles in
ferocious brown.

> "how She almost eloped home
> at 4
> and claustrophobic anticipation to run to the other side of the lake
> at 6.
> and then walk past street lamps growing out of rooms
> of special kids
> at 8."

frost chews red on her cheeks and sips lacrimals out of her eyes,
for breakfast and she lets it quench its thirst
every weekend morning.
Weekdays roast the tanned flesh out of handcrafted cardigans
in uniform fever.
When the broom in hand is to evacuate

spiders in countless concentration camps
allocated on a total of twenty-eight walls,
you stop wondering why clocks are lazy enough
or calendars too spendthrift.
the four long curtains gossip about
naphthalene balls rolling within
the layer of Banarasi silk threads.
She align the dust along the cashier doors just when
windows mock in her face the flattery of flowing time,
She'd mop lawns in a loop and footsteps would still
walk in like a never-ending playlist on shuffle.
Noon stretches its arm on the wide
window pane of her kitchen
and wet towel soak the broad border
in the wine-red glaze.

> "*promises made are jewellery in an open river,*
> *flashy and luring*
> *but also apparent and turbulent.*"

The alarm clock rubs its tantrums along her unkempt
hands lost in the search for silence.

> "*hopes tied to the threads of letters can often tie a relation with*
> *unbreakable string or often lead to strangling the letter itself.*"

when the lamps are low in the garden lights and stoves
roll up the sleeves for **adarak ki chai**
She packs the bag like an obedient woman
signs her register and leaves,

whilst the men slurp tea out of the perforated *kulhad.*
and laughter horizons the ending of women's day.

The adulting franchise

read them like a tarnished map of scavenger's hunt.

14. Zing-Girl Bells

the cabinets of voluble seats have a different accent
they talk on a low pitch and buffer on Sundays,
They skip the <u>multiple gaslighted stove I kindle</u>
with a monotonous keyboard covered in the saliva of a dry tongue.
my enchanted teeth, slip from a smile to an awkward memory,
that I make up really quick
and avoid conversation
with a still-life portrait of a teary eye looking
at the bright white pungent blank screen.
I peep through different corners, and call out fun names,
expecting the blue eyelids from some fancy store
would stop right in my direction and I will tell you,

> *"I wept kerosene for someone who paid some dollars for countable eyelids.*
> *when I chopped them to make a Kaleidoscope for your unemployed world."*

You could still see and so can I.
the world will look the same but with two different eyes,
as long as you settle the eyebrows on your forehead and admire
just anyone but me, it is fine.
I will still admire you because you wear the same
glossy eyelid as once I did, and please don't tell me,
I did not inspire you to buy them,

because that is the last eulogy I sang
for the few crumbs of indigo hair in the chestnut brown coffin box
of my eyelids.
But I don't look beautiful to the mirrors or to me, and I keep telling myself
that is *how a woman sings gender-specific serenades.*
with inkpot leaking down her dusky hands and the strings plucking her fingers.
I sleep with my cornea looking at the blunt foe from childhood,
stabbing knives into my hair braids that gradually disappear
to monopoly coins of heartbreak.
In the middle of the night, I irrigate my eyes with cold water that tastes saline and
leave the tap open as it keeps me company because yet
I find no buyer of the glass box I buried in the graveyard of my dark dollhouse.

I sit late comforting others,
with a lamp in my hand mining the right songs as it is dark behind the screen
and they ponder no bulbs
for the Christmas tree on the other side.
no matter how many smiling emoticons you put, they don't glow.
I try,
try to tell them the thirst that thinks teenage tastes tartaric,
and pour tequila into their champagne glasses,
To put them to sleep.
and vanquished glasses tell me they have been fed enough and I should stop trying in vain.

I cross calendar dates and calendar my talkative clothes,
for a busy eve that goes unnoticed and takes down the socks
off my fire alarm,
putting my tenebrous to sleep.
Mourning some menstrual cramps wakes me up and I sabotage myself with the
Champagne,
and collect my scrap of hair follicles from everywhere back to my hands, which reminds me of the frozen eyelids
that has bad breath and flushed cheeks.
So I should bury her uncostly demand with the zing-girl bells in the courtyard
that lost the ringing chamber to someone else's Xmas tree.
and plant the scavengers in some
the pensive post office where lives the dead letters of unacknowledged recipients with the
diary of the postmaster.
Feliz Navidad disappears in the background, now dead.

15. doors.

there are two sides of the door
and none of them belongs to us (me).
Inside,
stay the boomerangs hanging on highlights,
waiting for renewal.
The long lamps, hung low about to vanish,
to give new moments and moans some space.

    "we (I) never wanted."

There is a grass lawn, with endless fireflies
and the latest stock of winds,
where you won't suffocate and I won't battle
for more air to breathe.

    "'cause us (I) will be gone."

There are also some noodles left
in hot ceramic pots,
<u>I let you use as bait of sympathy for your next fish</u>
in midsummer pond.
Tell her, she left them and me in desolate state,
<u>with no arms to swim along my difficulties.</u>
The instruments in the corner,
loose strings often,
telling me to stop by, and unwind them

for another time.
but the count on the door is even,
and I was born on an odd date.
There are weak castles, blown away
in the air you both twirl now,
mostly stepping over its boundaries
or crashing upon them, in procedure
to find a place to make
love.
Yes, there is love inside and I am out of it.
The love that had my signature then,
and now mine epitaph devastated somewhere
in the corner.
Outside
it's me struck in the orbs
of never ending days,
and no silent nights.
all alone.
sliding three fingers over the broken screen,
preserving the death of some
laughs and sobs.
I wake up slightly when the doorbells chimes,
reminding I am not on the inner side,
even if the sun shines.
I greet faces similar enough, on the way across thresholds,
all happy and clandestine.
I feel like standing on the seashore, all decked up like
the silent utensils that make no noise,
and even silent pantry that haunts me

APARIGRAHA

With thuds of laughter, and grins on the limestone tiles.
I still feels your hands would entangle me your side
and tell me,
is our bond to weak for our odds and eves
or birthdates to decide its sacracy.
and I will grin widely to decline the truth.
Again.
I wish I could,

> "decline the truth, so as to be a little longer ."

16. Undress Hopes

I wore short sleeves in early February,
dancing barefoot upon the melting ice
celebrating the age long winters that ended between us.
Now doors will unlock ,
And so will the latches of your sun's cream
and talcum powder
with lots of moisture in the air.
in ripped jeans and crop tops,
when I heard you come out to loathe around in the sun.
With another hands to dance with
and another lips to talk.
Nothing seems familiar,
It is a cologne with a seduction in the air.
and heat like no other breeze will blow in.
Your hands,
draped in full sleeves of tericot white,
and breeches breach our contract of hot pants.
So should I turn around, walk again?
Should I stay by and look you fall into
shuffles of songs and maiden?
Or
Should I walk in with our playlist and broken headphones,
but then again
Will you wait for your turn?
or switch back to the new lyrics

of new songs. a new pair of ear plugs.
The moisture is high and bluish pink sky
winks at me with white fluffy clouds
and nostalgia aligns us together,
but

> "*Not every repetition is a happy poem*
> *and you won't look back*
> *or even stand by me.*"

I will walk to the edges where lies your part of the slam book
and think twice to tear it apart,
leaving it for the next day and make resolutions for
the new year that
begins every tomorrow.
I will overlap the mirrors upside down
and let them look at each other
like we did and the reflection smiled back.
It smiled but
I don't want everyone to weep with me.
Now I undress the cottons and fabrics of hopes,
the denim jeans
you told you can't take your eyes off
and silver glitters that bought you
peaceful chaos and gut flipping
excitement.
It is gone with the faded glitters.
and stinks with the sweat smell
and leftover perfume of teenage days that now blooms

like an adult.

17. Hi College Days

-for all those countless times, I still count on you -
Meanwhile, the lightening and thunder
will rest in peace, I want to stable
myself upon a calming sea shore
of unattended waves.
Alas! The suburban beds with ugly
mess waits for me
both tired and disappointed
to carry the load for long.

> "and the silence in me
> stealthily waits for you to show up."

The make up goes too heavy to droop my skin
down to earth and the light ones
evaporates into air of mysoginitic eyes
The shades and bamboo long
heels do comply with
silver folds and jelly on my lips

> "the face, though repels your shade
> but perfection can't slay without you."

A sip of silence glares through the rule book
of warden, the unwanted notice

and dubious false promises
to enchant us and complete your
absolute absence.
little did she know,
choking on smiles and dieing to laugh
isn't what apricity of motherly sunshine
looks like.
I celebrated it well,
with sequence of
dress, dj, dance and drama
So they left after
bells were dead and doesn't chimes
anymore.
And big day is over

> "*vacant enough for your hugs*
> *bleeding weeds out on the cheeks*
> *that you kissed to wake up everyday.*"

Another December winds knock the door
and Redstart left hold on them quite soon
with no reminder to fix
the windowpane that permeates
abandoned winds to gossip about the
morning quarrels of my fluttering hands
to shut up the inhumane alarm

> "*unlike your soft touch and*
> *an argument to stay in a little more.*"

So I pack up with my damp fidgeting fist
blotted in ink
toxic enough to swallow the meal

> "*and no tender hands*
> *To feed me the lunch for I'm tired*
> *and my nap disobeys the growls of*
> *empty stomach.*"

I bid you another painful smiling
Adieu!

18. LONELINESS

So we box up ourselves with some sympathy stuffed in brain,
for loneliness is in the
cold walls
empty rooms
and a few people to ponder thoughts about you
with the love leftover in their crockery of life.
Seriously?
Let's see.
In your teens, when others were dressing crazy for prom nights and
farewell dates, choosing
the perfect elegant pair of wedge heels
matching with their pitch dark golden black net sarees.
and you honour yourself to the bed beside your sibling,
curling up for its still winter for you in
luke warm February beds.
You fake snores for the lights off and the two elders
on nearby beds, whisper softly
about aunt next door.
Its still not midnight, the whispers are dead,
and an imperfect silence.
Repercussive moist sobs, that skips your heart
unwillingly,
only to vanish in the inland drainage of quilts.
The air of loneliness smothers your nostrils
everytime you inhale the environment you survive in.

and its toxicants irritate you next morning
when you attend the familiar faces.
The puffed up eyes dense like clouds on monsoon nights,
dark and heavy
about to droop anytime now.

> "*Every next day pass and unfolds the sleeves*
> *little by little*
> *looking at the wardrobe you once despised to choose.*"

Often, I pass the glass mirror etched to modern grills of my house
or sometimes pity myself looking at the irregular reflection
from the springs by the oak trees for free minds to bathe,
and I'm one locked in the four by four
rooms, somewhere at my deep self
I fear the shallow ends too.
There's a black cotton wall between badmintons and breasts
that grew with grewing age,

> "*too high*
> *for any shuttle cock to drop by chance*
> *on my side.*"

Now you see I'm homogeneous to all the sugar molecules
growing with me
and somewhere lost in the sugar of this tasteless world.
Repeating cycles and beating both hind and fore limbs
to never let the paddles stop.
Draping a costly silk cloth, the most dull, I could ever buy

to fit in the ambassadors of sober diesel.
I own a watch
that's too heavy and too slim to pierce the needles
of time well into the
blotting veins.
Outside is a cool breeze and inside is warmth with a junior
and two seniors
like on the teenage nights.
Certain days back to home, bangles wave at me
pondering problems of
my *l o n e l i n e s s*
for which I don't seek answers even after
excelling in every grades.
The nights dress me in another peach dress,
the decent as it could ever be upon a bed
okay for still still okay
for I live with adrenaline too.
Fame looks at the window and peace stings through the slits
wrapped in the moonlights
even sneeze don't fetch me a bad luck
so that I could cry for reasons.
I should rather end or let you pity more
but the truth is,
with all in hand and nothing
more to get
am I sufficiently incomplete, or incompletely sufficient
drools my lips looking at the principles
that never tasted street food
and the principles mock me,

'cause I never tasted them either.

19. Have you ever been drenched in tension of desperate rains?

On the lopsided islands that *stays* in the temple under
monochromatic polyester house,
both desperate and desolate to
seek visitors soon.
Growing circles out of circles
for a welcome feast that
Neither looks perfect nor real.
and still the oars of impatience glide
stroke after stroke
in the false center of concentric caves.
The shores left open prepare
trumpets from vocals and look
with triumph all over vanishing in
thuds of mocking sea,
crushing the nerves of an unattended echo
Sheepishly rebounding forever.
The silver braids of some Inko-minko trees
short of existence anywhere else,
swing along, walking hand in hand
as if they will overcome the trade of happiness
over fancy or feisty tables,
when likewise(trees) in this world barely walk

and unlike here they don't play
Red-hands with weathering leaves.
And when the winds unsettle at the dock,
the perennial horses and cavalry
summersaults from cloud to cloud
in the tiresome scripts of welcome speech
but

"*<u>Rehearsals of never happening events are just the perfect descendants of false hopes.</u>*"

cropping of the reigns for future horses to the forest of hallucinations
where witches ride the logs of judgment called prejudice
at arrivals of unicorns and reindears.
The tree house is locked within
woods of narcotic breeze
are breathing through the tallest exit of the shortest doors
keeping the peals of laughter of every color alive
while the rest few at the outskirts are rusted
in all shades of dark, dead, and grey.
Manufacturing smokes of morphine to
chambers of memory-making rolls.
Not to forget teaching clouds to look scenic by wearing umbrellas of
all faithful colors and leaving the neck unguarded
for hills to carve into
bodylicious pulps, fragile but appealing.
and walking winds with saddles in hand and apron around the neck
to favor the odds of visitors.
which becomes odder.

And when nothing works,
planting allies of promise none can keep,
like a peninsula with water on no side
and young mountains with diverging tectonic plates
And a lot like a confused sea with no meanders
as if sapiens never traded their nerves before.

"*Sleep never comes easy with the perfection of*
Scarlets and rose beads knitted in the tiara of
A 10 o'clock night.
"

And somehow the autotrophy begins,
cooking fuels with vanilla scented tears and corundum
in peanut oil.
Under an open sky of calamities,
to spice the dinner,
the clouds burst drop by drop puking
Open-mouthed salamanders on the sour grounds of dead wishes.
nibbling meniscus on the sand,
that doesn't disappear at all,

"*gradually freezing the water on all sides for visitors seeking*
an off winter sale."

20. If it were my last poems

"but culprits, my child, culprits don't chew lips and weep the inks of forgiveness before lords of the one with the pants on shall be forgiven.
"

It is three in the morning
way too late and way too early
for supper as it lays fast asleep
open to the air, cuddling with crockery
for warmth in expensive winter rains.
The wind chime is still calling
someone unknown for help.
while *the claustrophobic footprints,*
the profane smell of chocolates
mixed in the saliva of used <u>syndromes,</u>
forges virginity in a new bloodbath.
The iron door was petrified in blood clots
and guilt trips,
slammed a hundred times
with voluble,
very voluble ignorance
running drills between the pantry
and house bills, dressing charades
for some distant kith and kin

and refunding happiness in envelopes
of snowflake currencies and costly brocaded tuxedos.
The footsteps however listen through the door and postpone the knock
For some idle days perhaps

> "*the sobs of one's child are futile ways to use time.*"

Occasionally, I could eat the bone china ice bowls and look into the eyes of dead stars but today they are blurry and I would love to swallow a few warmer hugs.
and drink words that could heal my sore throat and please my chastened lips.

21. Nothing hurts me anymore

The limpid desire to sit by the long-gone cotton fields with naked love for weathering pollen, stolen by winds on an occasional sinister love scene. I envy them, their flaccid innocence that has no decisions.

How often do I sit with parchments and ink pots snailing ink on the nostrils of pen quill, writing stories where two people, sometimes a duplet of men or a couple of women, sniffing the fresh clothes out of the watermelon tubs, snaking the arms and water together at the edge of a freshwater river, blooming sprinklers for farmers at a different edge to ripe the fields dwelled with the love of two valentines? Never, so said the winds that bother to upturn the curtains, they peek at my empty wooden skin, clean as ever, and the Parthian leather bloats with the stigma of an ink drop relinquished by dried pen quills.

How often do I buy the ball pens and Tsai Lun's pot meal to script a puppet show that is desperate to talk of two lovers, of which one dances the footsteps of "Oh Rangeela re" while the other holds the drumbeats in a long kurta-pajama and partly distributed hair hidden behind the hill caps? Never, so said the man with white whiskers and polished lens resting upon his frowning nose with rusted lips chewing leftover slides of tobacco left in his life.

How often do I sit with the bird who located her perch at my defeated, bygone windows and record the scenes of the pink sky that sells candy floss to the umbrellas dancing in rain for hours till it is time for the traffic lights where hide a lot of blistered faces like me hiding behind sunglasses during night time? Never, so says the feathers of the flop on my windows for hours and retrieve, accepting defeat.

How often do I suck the blood out of an uneven thumb that bled salt after strangling in between the spacebar of a nonchalant typewriter wearing no courtesy to switch positions at the endpaper rolls and move ahead as I should? Never, so says the drops of endless blood drops forming cobweb after cobweb around the same wound that doesn't clot.

How often do I clap my tongue with an empty mug and sigh in the direction of a dead stove, unlike the adjacent room that I am describing? Never, so says the cursor standing still and blinking at the home of my end.

Yes, Never. Nothing hurts me anymore. It should not because on January nights I chose to close the winds of ghastly sunshine at four o'clock in the dilemma if it is evening or noon. I packed the tamarinds in a bottle full of happiness and said freezing is but an art of science. So now it doesn't hurt me anymore as long as it is an idle night or the Ides of March, that leaves behind me and Calpurnia alone on a paper in two different time zones.

How may I put this?

this turmoil, it sits in me like a winter guest.

22. Immortal Death

It's long to tell, I'll summarise some day,
before I die of living guilt
All I recall is the black bower of arrows
veiling the azure sky,
red lake plating over black terrain
The squalor that smelt of human blood
and birds that sang, songs of fireworks
The swords playing hide and seek
with every valor now and then,
Then a few more, more minutes I was surprised,
Something curbing my throats
Twisting my guts
talking to me of Halloween nights
Then surpassed my dear zones
The embrace of love
The ache in the limbs of my genitor
The blue innocence of lady born.

-And -

and a mirror
that told
It's mortal for all
and unpredictable for you
'cause triggers don't recoil

APARIGRAHA

and decide once left,
They escape the metallic case
Taking immortal death

23. Bloated Letters

Bloated letters
covet of December isles kissed the sheriff's
dainty letters arched like the boats
on the seashore of morphine.
greasing the edges,
painting algae.
E n v e l o p e s
sinking in tequila, and torqouise tears
till sobs consume the blurred vision
of unattended lover who unattended the
bloated letters.

24. How may I put this?

Dearest you,
Hope this letter finds you alive.

> "*and so like the other five incomplete battles I will rip off the sixth one too into a paper plane that crash lands the window in an off winter rain.*
>
> *And there goes another, maybe to be a paper plane, plain beneath my hands.*"

Dearest you,
Hope this letter rides to you while it is young and white enough with my cologne. I wish you smile back like it is a birthday present and you are still as old as our boy.
Standing young with an empty hand in the pocket of a neatly ironed coat and other painting toposheet red and blue.

> "*Do smile back with happiness and not pain, do not pretend either, I know how much heavier the jaw line sinks when you smile with a load of all tears aligned.*"

And right now I am jealous of my own fragrance that will rest for a day in his vest pocket, beside the soft beats of a rigid heart.
How have you been all these days?
No letters, no news, no victory tales.
Things are pretty good here.

"*And now begins the series of lies.*"

I got a better job last week,
everyone at home is alright.
We all love you and it has been very long since you have written to us.
Yes of course, his mother wakes up with rosary beads and still forgets the count every five minute and recounts the count of hundred and eight, a hundred more times.
The glasses are so dipped in frost even in spring that his dad holds his long childhood album and reads the faces like an unread mythology every time. Our boy debates between what is right and what is wrong and now makes decisions like me. I wish he won't be cross with his son when they next meet before the television screen at eight in the evening with a debate over ice hockey as I do.
Else what should I quote that every screeching rickshaw puller that drops by in the neighbourhood, makes me look out of the window and find the same jersey but different eyes and hairs and fixtures and simply not him.
Okay now that is possible only if someday he calls to inform that he isn't cancelling the holiday for the coming month.
I guess you are alright and nothing disturbs you at all. If in thicks and thins there becomes any chances for you to visit us, please do come.
Before dad forgets you completely and our boy doesn't know you at all. There are days I strive to smile and also forget that I am smiling or my face is curled up in a look.
Waiting for you to write back soon.
Right back now!

Ageing climbers

it crawls your skin every night and grips your the chair's arm till it stops rocking forever.

Timer never rings as fast as the alarm clock does.

25. Woods by lake

In the woods by lake
that fire in the dark and
Cerise sunshine
scattering its warmth

Holy land aren't consecrated
with hazardous lapse
for a dekas beauty now
I realise

The antiphons of holts
aren't painted green
There verses are red
and voices sanguine

26. Epiphany is Waiting

Is it all about borrowed emotions?
Yes, it is.
if ever I had voice
I would have not wasted
my inks to keep the **debris alive**.
Things happen,
and miseries are flushed by the fleeting wheels of time.
Do they?
Isn't it a cassette that you rewind when on a cool day,
A breeze soaks your sweat and odors are attending their funeral,
a small leaf caresses the lower of your back and you twist over your ankles.
Why?
Is your wheel taking a back turn down the road of your memory lane?
Is the cassette not fixed? Did you not bury it?
What collapses the same happy-go-lucky portrait you portray to everyone?
Is the chivalry of knife sleeping with blood lately?
Did someone keep the ballet wait for years under the mistletoe?
Epiphany awaits, every Saturday at the dockyard of sweating shirts
with
A noose knot tied in kern mantle rope.
still, waiting!

27. Can you sing me some new metaphors please?

Rocking armchairs, swings late every nights
Leftovers and liquors play chaotic fights
Elegantly my wrinkles laugh at self

Telling the mauve ancient covers
To hold on, the doodles scribbling lovers
'cause giant track slay and I lie as mere elf

My autographs go back to signatures
My poetries feel less, dumb caricatures
A petrichor then, now a bygone smell

So I keep things and alchohol at bay,
Trying to smile a little each day
Painting new poems upon broken sea shells

Replying to queries that hit deep ashore
"Can you please sing me some new metaphors?"

28. Balls and Chains

poetry(she/her)
Still they try,
her brand new lung that could not even breathe to respire and exhale
o x y g e n
plenty of oxygen
that would last forever.
What if it doesn't?
What if it forgets the process and
Dies?
A neat white envelope will slip into her rusted box,
upon the brickwall holding age long iron gates.
Because forks and notes never get rusted,
and that will whiten your white napkins
When you savour the sour sausage over inescapable molecules struck
in alveoli.
When she walks in those exceptionally high and glassy slippers,
with a tint of cliche
in rose gardens, because her devil can still breathe.
and one can't tie the entire lawn into
balls and chains, but in words
a Galaxy.
One doesn't need surgery knives, when the heart belongs to Saudade.
It can be ripped off any time,
with some claws that jibes right at the wrong spots.
What long band aids would one cover her scars with,

**the silk will spread the blood in community,
and raincoats will be too opaque to hide
the communist thighs.**
Will you let it bleed to death, rather?
May be the pain of survival would hurt more,
but then what will bring you diamond knifes to drill through the
undead again.
She has less of blood left,
and more of open ended wound to swallow
like spices on a half cut tongue
that smells its own lungs and talk of its own adrenalin.
How one taught her to wear the garbedines and smile like maiden's
and then tell her not fear the broken nips and green pen,
It felt like a thousand spiders built an empire for the rest your life when
eulogies will read
still with an unbandaged
and diamond pierced figurine walking in with naked wounds
Spilling blood drops on the yet alive epitaph,
When would it die?
When the oxygen escapes the alveoli
Or when blood swamps
freeze to reciprocate.
And just in case it makes you feel any better.
it hurts
that poetry is a Godess and Goddess don't die.

29. Sublimed Graves

With ending noons, I will sleep there
with eyelids crawling backward and lips
welcoming a lion back to the den like a daunting
danger sign board with a pale face and wrinkled nose.
What thoughts would fetch my naps when I should be wide awake,
stitching napkins.
Will I think of it coming or will I recall the thoughts I am thinking now?
I must be old then, Very old.
like the brown shacks raised to be a tavern with roofs.
The big rich tavern and earthquakes swallow them back,
and so do the giant hands of the clock
circling the brown Iets, turning white with every name.
Every new name.
What song would I listen to?

> "*The old barber on the road,*
> *off to the hillside.*
> *With grandsire on the rockbed,*
> *what else the sons decide.*"

Or

> "*On the rustdoors,*
> *with cardamoms and breadcrumbs*
> *We'll sit on the wrong talks*

and disappear with pools
In the back water of warm thumbs."

Or

"Will you still disrobe the fantasies,
and sing me the fairy tales.
With blindfolds and red drapes,
we will swallow the naked whales.
Will you still disrobe the fantasies,
with wrong rings on the stakes,
And sail off on the ships with me,
that takes us to happy waves."

Or
I would swallow counters and cabinets, burning radios on the tip
of the *pinhole camera*.
And that again brings me to wonder,
what will happen next?
What second name will these graves be addressed with?
What if the future hunts me with a wild knock
on the wooden unlike mine Iron planks.
What will be the scales of the death in the freshman daily press,
will anyone come to cross-check
or will I sit and die and melt into the salts of the sublime grave?
Graves with nothing but soil, and lots of useless air to breathe.
Lots of fresh grass to decay with and lots of forgetfulness
to mix in the soil that was not meant to be fertile.
Who will declare the dead is dead, and who will weep me to the new life,

who will sit around and mile behind the tears and pretend to sob endlessly?
Who will repaint the large villa I will leave behind
or what will be the name of the new rich tavern mee,
Which earthquake will swallow it back?
Tring Tring...
'I received the rent. Thanks.'
There it goes, the weeping hands of a clock that tells me to find
just another sublime grave
and in time.

30. In standstill backwaters of past

It is like my boat is arched at the edge
I wanted,
but loneliness shares my oar.
The waters startle my eyes every time
I ponder its brilliance
snapshots of sailing ships pierce through
my naked visions.
Smiles of every other lip
curves mine to a different trip of
soulfulness.
Back again to the square zero
with rusted glitters of limestones.
Chopped of wrinkles
and overly done scratches that pinch
every corner of my eyes.
Dance of decades dance for coming
centuries and much more to pass by.
Greens by the silt of deceptive memories
stand straight, about march past over another
epitaph, I will sign in my name.
Fine arts of deception overgraze my shallow seeds
of patience,
fertilizing pollen of insecurity.
And weeds, closing eyes to survive.

APARIGRAHA

No death, not alive.

31. farehenheit

I don't know what hurts more. Deja vu or stagnant stinking water. We can pull out our wet sweaters from the pond and wash them anytime with the petals of all worldly possessions, but can we stop smelling the odor of the stinking rafflesia blooming ironically at some distance and we are beaming back at it?

We are trapped, we all are. At a point you sit down cross-legged with a bunch of notes in one hand and miss the empty ink pots, also the time you used to miss the filled ones, sitting in between the cushions of warm hands and discussing how much you missed them and that you were spoiled by the comfort. Now, what spoils you? The unorganized beds? The cold threshold of your vacant room, the strangling rope hanging down the well across the road. <u>The silent cell phone that wakes you up but forgets to put you back to sleep.</u>

We all play the same songs and decipher different meanings of every line we read and make castles in the air and breathe marks on the wine glasses, we would dress up in the same lime sneakers and high ponytails for a morning walk which was once a prologue of an ended relationship. And when all the strange faces would look back with crawling smiles we would reply the tears off to our eighth floor, deceiving the self-realization of how much we are struck by the candlelight dinners that ended up sleeping with cold foods and spilled wines.

We campaign against our urge to sit back straight and scroll down the photos that look a lot like ones kept in a storeroom with broken frames and bleeding glasses, and also the same photos you took down from the screensaver of your cell phone. You will walk to the basin with fingers looking for a toxic dose of relationship and eyes searching for a soothing gaze to cure feverish skin. An ayurvedic gaze, with no side effects and toes, stop working at the sight of a half-broken cup that once chipped your lips for being honest and went down your esophagus as a lesson to lie forever, but how far did your forever last itself?

Songwriters are born every month. Somewhere in the dumb corner of the world, someone is hoping to see you soon, in just the way you are, so just hug the stinking sweater and let it dry. Take it off, sleep naked within the covers of white bedsheets and brown blankets, and let the wounds heal. Let them wrap the winter and stitch yourself some fabrics lighter than cotton. The summers have a lot of sweat to breathe the lemons of your skin.

32. Death

I'm dead,
All aligned by white stumps
and I, The Queen amid them.
Draped in florals, red
and vibrant brocades.

With my eyes closed I see
sun silk rays kissing
me on all sides
but the passion of cuddle is dead
the rays aren't warm anymore

My olfactory fades away
vacates my nerves
My daughter sprays the cologne
neither my nose
nor my skin can remember

I feel numb by this point of time
I see with closed eyes
No smell, I can encounter
I read the cologne and remember not
I touch the flower
void of strength pretty much
I hear nothing

like vacuum around me
and I am in Universe

I see them
They see me
They feel me and I can not

And the sun that bids Bye
It dawned on me
I'm me and not me
In struggle see the pile of sticks
wavering to me
Evading mantras that chant
Fire ready to explode me
I see
I revise
I can't breathe
I can't survive

The bed by the lake of winters
In dumb vacuum

Ain't either good in this land
Or in lands of infinity

Finally, that fire derived
Out of me a scream
A scream back to life
In the softness of the mattress
Draping the cotton fabric
Soaked in the slumber of sweat
With eyes wide alive all open
Nostrils with the warmth of breath
Suns that fondle its rays down to me
Showering love and not cold flames
I see
I revise
I'm wide awake
for I'm alive.

I painted a picture, the picture was a painting of you-Aurora.

If things weren't happening around me, I would never be able to paint a picture of it, agreed? Through Poetry like Marriages, ***Once upon a time, I met a Future Rapist***, Ars Moriendi, and The Badnaam Gali, I have tried my best to portray the picture of the issues we live every day yet don't talk about or discuss. In the poem, "Was I painting the petals of petroleum coasted flowers,?" Itra, To dust-Holic almirah, Zing- Girl Bells, I pulled out little efforts to channelize the anger towards the ultimate bad and take the burden off the shoulders of humans in our life, whom we judge or take for granted like we have the liberty to.

Feel free to contact me at jaggerywrites@gmail.com or drop your reviews in the message section of my Instagram handle @justjaggerythings. I am willing to listen to all valuable suggestions from my readers and work on them. I am grateful for the time you all have invested in my book. The most satisfying feeling in the world is to be heard and have people around who are willing to acknowledge how you feel.

Aparigraha

Closure, an act or process of closing something, especially an institution, thoroughfare, or frontier, or of being closed. Leaving behind the poetry I am holding close to me for 3-4 years now.

    I was told, my work is long and confusing, also that I shouldn't write on the subjects that are beyond my approach. Honestly, I know maybe I am just trying too hard but also one day Esha said to me,"Just play with it, do what makes you happy." so I thought twice and this book with its errors and confusions, make me happy. Teena said, "You write good, you should put it out for the world to read." and rolled my sleeves to work hard enough on the book. Manjeet ma'am out of blue said to me,"You have a nice hobby, keep it going and make me proud." I wish I could make you and all my teachers from primary, junior and senior wing of LPS Anand Nagar proud. I am honestly so overwhelmed to have people in my life who keep pushing me to work in the direction. Sharma, Sarthak, Kundan and Dodo, my little anti depressants always cheering me up. Thank you for existing you little fools.

    Thank you so much to my Teachers and Professors for contributing to my growth. My whole hearted thanks to my seniors for approvals and juniors for the energy.

When love sleeps, does it dreams of us?
it does, it does, it does

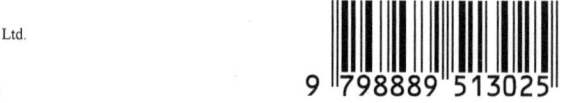

so I still look at the peach rocks and the abandoned paintings of an adolescent. they have one thing in common, two people walking a long ru in still pictures.

and I plagiarise the iconic shararat on their lips and wear it beneath the night suits after brushing the corners with the most costly mouthwash.

But I sleep unlike them.

~Jaya Chaudhary

ISBN 979-888951302-5